# CATS

CATS of ASIA

NORTHERN LYNX

WILDCAT

of EUROPE

SNOW LEOPARD

FISHING CAT

PALLAS'S CAT

CARACAL

CHEETAH

CLOUDED LEOPARD

LEOPARDS

LION

of AFRICA

SERVAL

CARACAL

CHEETAH

SACRED CAT

TIGER

LEOPARDS

PERSIAN
(ANGORA)

SIAMESE

*of the* AMERICAS

CANADA LYNX

BOBCAT

PUMA

NORTH *of the* RIO GRANDE

JAGUARS

*and*
*mostly* SOUTH
*of the*
RIO
GRANDE

JAGUARUNDI

MARGAY

OCELOT

PUMA

PAMPAS CAT

NOT ALL
MY RELATIVES ARE
SHOWN ····· HERE.

THERE ARE OVER 40 DIFFERENT KINDS OF CATS.

WSB

# CATS

Written and Illustrated by
## WILFRID S. BRONSON

SUNSTONE
PRESS

SANTA FE

Sunstone books may be purchased for educational, business, or sales promotional use. For information please write: Special Markets Department, Sunstone Press, P.O. Box 2321, Santa Fe, New Mexico 87504-2321.

Library of Congress Cataloging-in-Publication Data

Bronson, Wilfrid S. (Wilfrid Swancourt), 1894-
  Cats / written & illustrated by Wilfrid Swancourt Bronson.
    p. cm.
  Originally published: New York, 1950.
  ISBN 978-0-86534-645-1 (softcover : alk. paper)
  1. Cats–Juvenile literature.  I. Title.

SF445.7.B76 2008
636.8–dc22

                          2007051005

Published in

WWW.SUNSTONEPRESS.COM
SUNSTONE PRESS / POST OFFICE BOX 2321 / SANTA FE, NM 87504-2321 /USA
(505) 988-4418 / ORDERS ONLY (800) 243-5644 / FAX (505) 988-1025

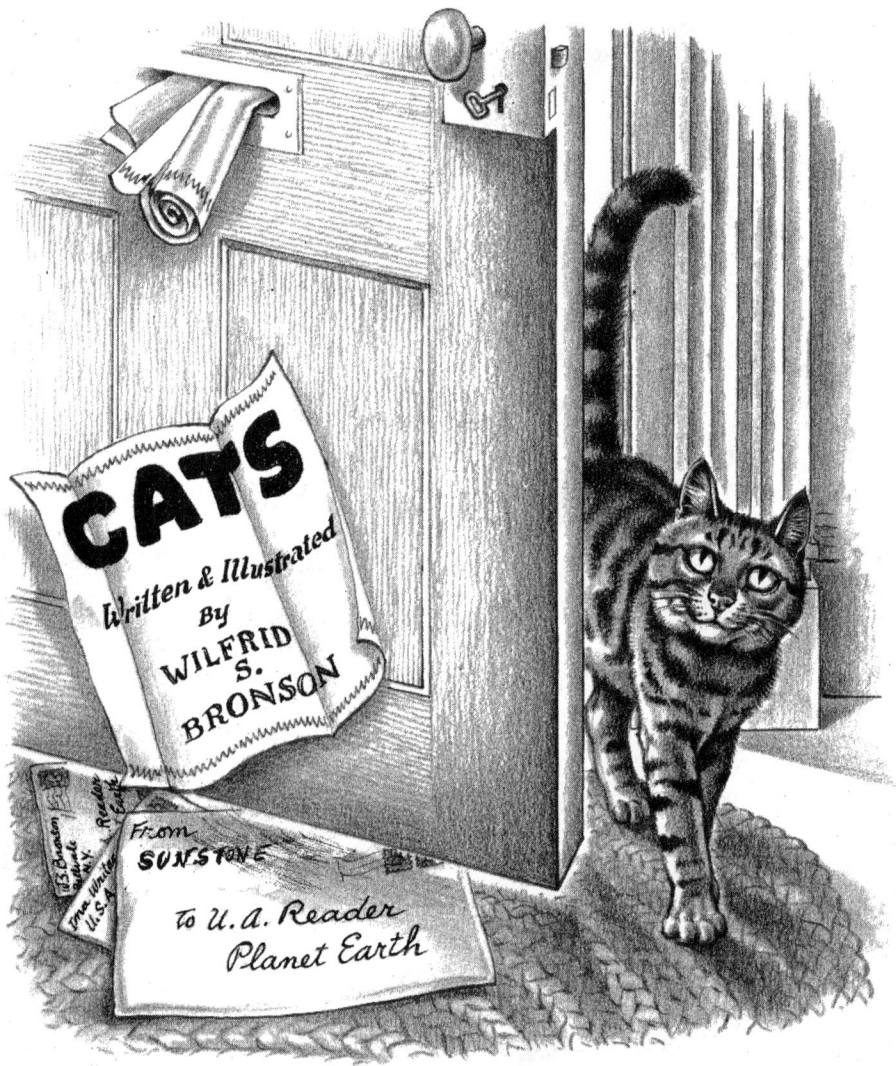

ARTIFICIAL COMB & BRUSH added to Kitty's natural ones.

I'VE NEVER SEEN A REAL MOUSE. BUT I CAUGHT A COCKROACH ONCE, AND AT LEAST THIS FISH IS REAL!

KARE for KATS

"FEE-LINE" fodder Special

GRASS SEED

CATNIP SEED

MADE BY MAKE-BELIEVE MOUSE-HOLE CO.

TOY MOUSE

PING-PONG

WSB

FISH FOOD

COD LIVER OIL

MINERAL OIL

WORM-GO PILLS

FLEA FLEE

IMITATION TREE TRUNK

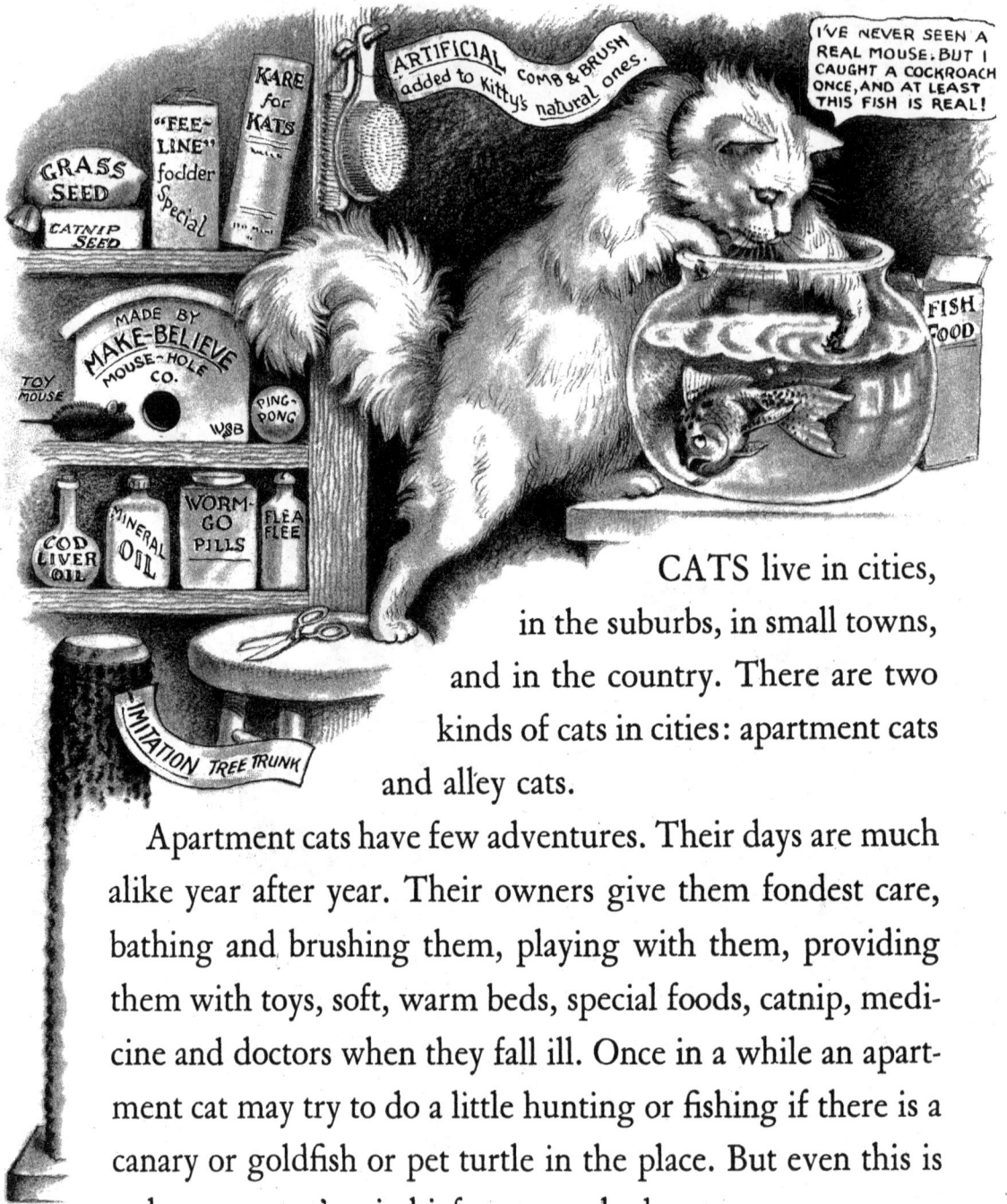

CATS live in cities, in the suburbs, in small towns, and in the country. There are two kinds of cats in cities: apartment cats and alley cats.

Apartment cats have few adventures. Their days are much alike year after year. Their owners give them fondest care, bathing and brushing them, playing with them, providing them with toys, soft, warm beds, special foods, catnip, medicine and doctors when they fall ill. Once in a while an apartment cat may try to do a little hunting or fishing if there is a canary or goldfish or pet turtle in the place. But even this is only a moment's mischief, not a real adventure.

Alley cats often have too many adventures. Nearly nobody knows what happens to them, and very few people care. While apartment cats are leading their tame, protected lives, alley cats crawl in and out of garbage cans in dingy back yards, dirt alleys, and dark cellars, cold, wet and filthy, often ill, dodging traffic, dogs, and people, safe nowhere, trusting no one, and almost as wild as the city rats and mice they prey on.

But the true nature of both kinds of city cats is one-half tame and one-half wild. So, since one kind gets all comfort but no adventure, while the other gets all adventures and no comfort, neither is really satisfied. For both are living only half a cat's good life.

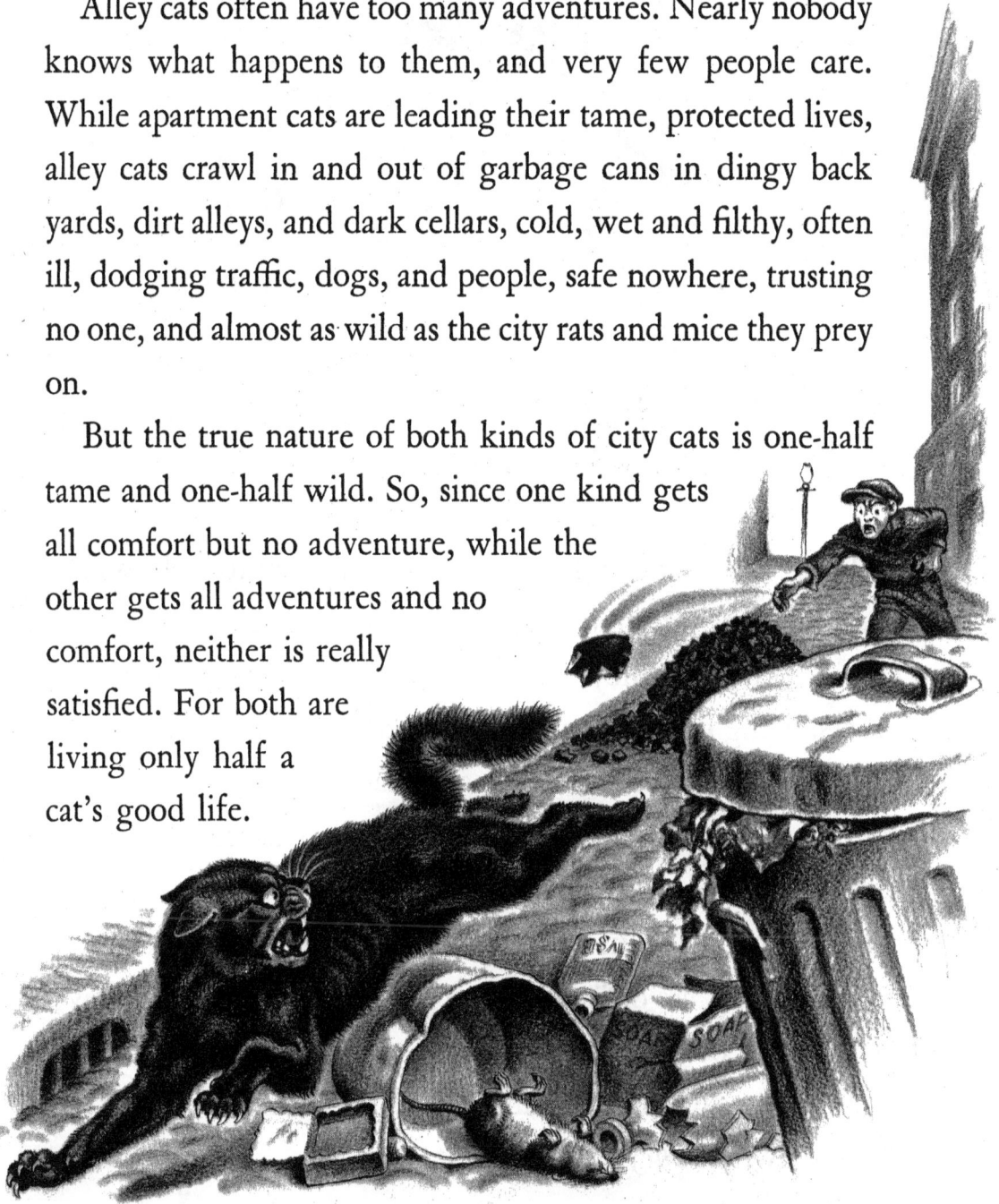

Three kinds of cats live in the country: completely wild ones, barn cats, and house cats. The wild ones are the country cousins of the city alley cats. Some are born in the woods, but others, living there, have been deserted by their owners. Perhaps they all are better off than alley cats, living as they do in the great clean out-of-doors. But they likewise have to live entirely by their wits on whatever they can catch. Nobody feeds them milk or luscious cat-foods. The only cushions they lie on are of grass or leaves on sunny days. And always they must watch out for dangerous wild animals as well as dogs and hunters. For many hunters will shoot any cat they see hunting where *they* want to hunt.

Barn cats have the comfort and security of a haymow and a steady job. They work at keeping rats and mice out of the stored grain and feed. Their pay is milk, all they can hold. But no other food is offered, for few farmers realize that good mousers will hunt just as hard for fun, after a full meal, as they will when hungry. Barn cats get very little fondling from busy milkmen, and farmers' wives never let them into the house.

Some drink milk from a pan, but many learn to take it from "the fountain".

The cats which really have full, satisfying lives are the house cats, kept as pets, whether they live in the country, in small towns, or in the suburbs of cities. These cats keep houses and gardens free from mice, but spend much of the day sleeping indoors on our best furniture or on their own special beds by stoves or radiators. They are given good regular meals of milk, cat-foods and table scraps right in the kitchen. They roost in people's laps, are loved and petted and played with. All day long they make people let them in and out until the last time just before the family goes to bed. These are the cats that get everything out of life that they are able to enjoy. For after a safe and pleasant day of ease and tameness, they step out into the night to live the other half, the thrilling wild half of their lives.

THERE IS ONLY THE THICKNESS OF THE DOOR BETWEEN HIS TWO NATURES.

Suppose we are letting our cat Tom, a tabby, out for the night. While the door is closing he is changing from a tame to a wild animal. From now till sunrise, he will be living as dangerously as any wild cat of the woods, strictly on his own.

African wild-dogs hunting antelope

He takes a step only when the rabbit takes a mouthful.

But that is how he wants it. Unlike a dog (which likes to have other dogs, or his master, or the whole family, with him on his rambles), a cat wants to hunt by himself. For millions of years it has been this way—wolves and dogs hunting noisily in packs, mostly by day, cats hunting noiselessly alone, mostly at night. Dogs can chase the game for hours till they tire it out. Cats must creep close enough to catch it in one jump.

*TOP VIEW of a Cat in a pitch-dark tunnel—*

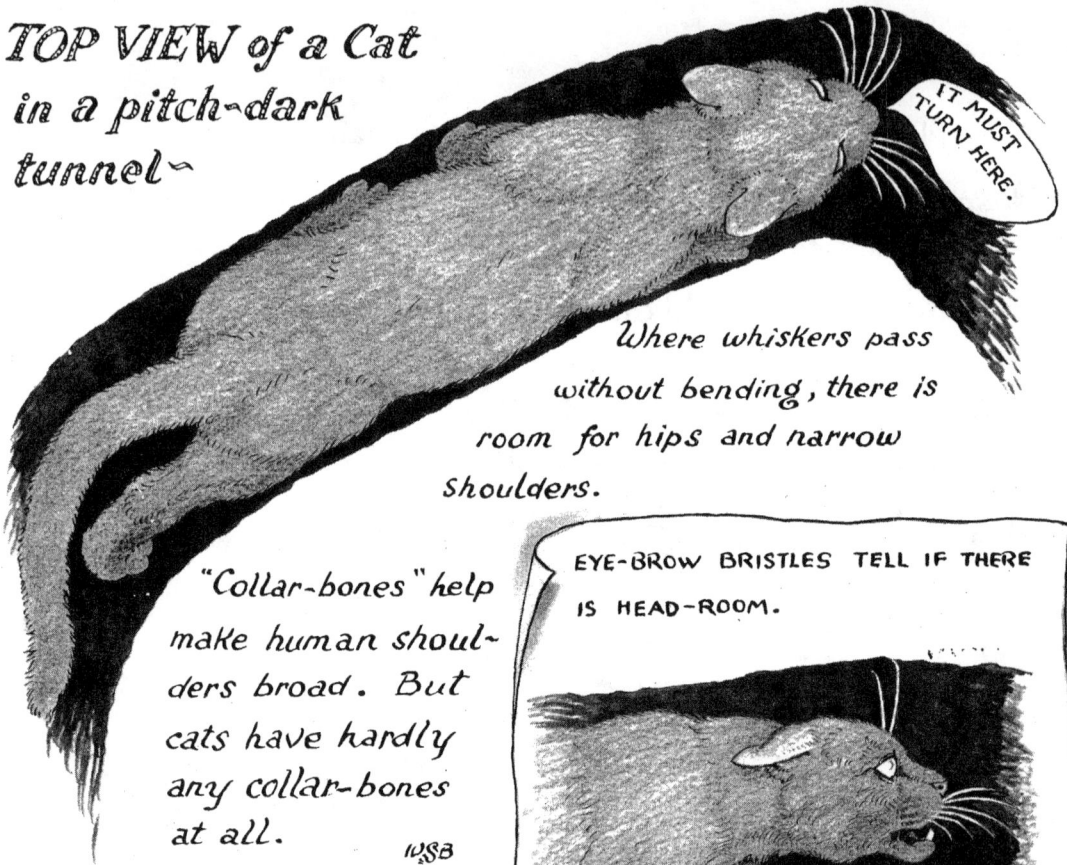

IT MUST TURN HERE.

*Where whiskers pass without bending, there is room for hips and narrow shoulders.*

*"Collar-bones" help make human shoul-ders broad. But cats have hardly any collar-bones at all.*

WSB

EYE-BROW BRISTLES TELL IF THERE IS HEAD-ROOM.

After dark a cat's long stiff whiskers, fanning out before and on both sides of his face, help him to keep from bumping into things or getting into tangled places. He feels his way with his whiskers. At the same time he feels for firm footing with his padded forepaws. Deftly he sets them down, disturbing no loose stick or stone, making no slightest sound.

The soft pads are full of tender nerves for feeling surfaces.

They are also full of fat, which helps keep them warm in winter.

4 feet leave only 2 prints ~

His hind feet step exactly in his forepaws' tracks. Thus silently he moves through darkest woods, dense underbrush, or meadow weeds and grasses.

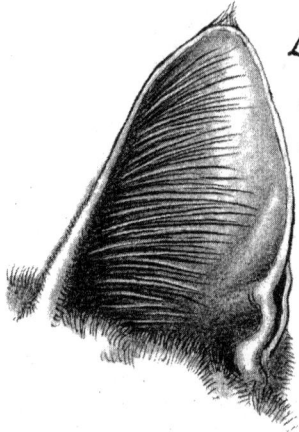

Long, stiff hairs in the scoop, like a cluster of auto radio antennae ~

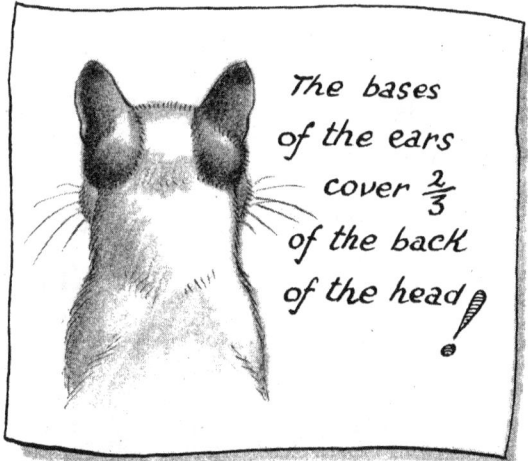

The bases of the ears cover $\frac{2}{3}$ of the back of the head!

The cat's keen ears are like big sound-scoops on his head. They funnel every tiniest noise into his brain. At night, out in the meadow, the weakest squeak tells him where to watch for the mice he already smells. And he can see a good deal in

**SIDE VIEW INSIDE A CAT'S EYE**

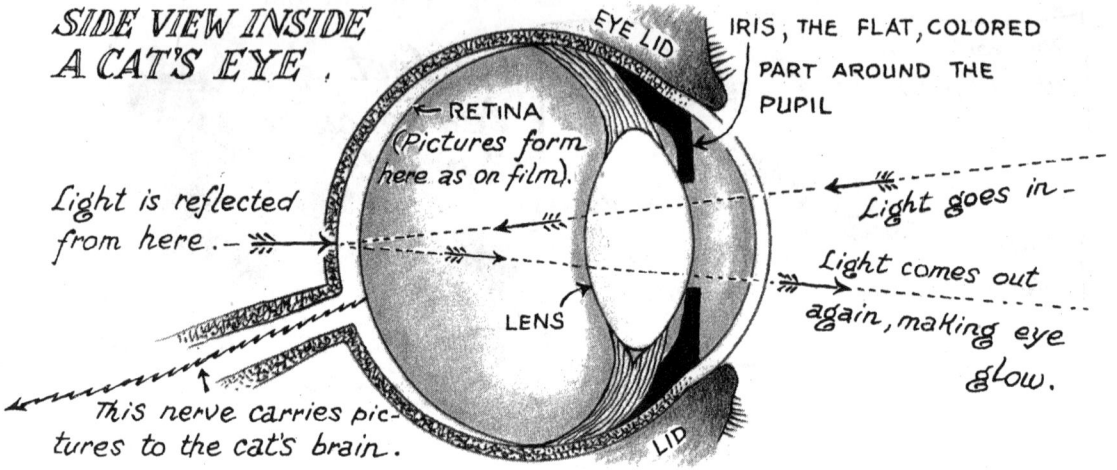

EYE LID

IRIS, THE FLAT, COLORED PART AROUND THE PUPIL

← RETINA (Pictures form here as on film).

Light is reflected from here. →

Light goes in →

← Light comes out again, making eye glow.

LENS

This nerve carries pictures to the cat's brain.

LID

---

the darkness too, if only by the light from a few faint stars. For his eyes make double use of whatever light there is, collecting and reflecting it before him like two tiny flashlights.

An eye is a living camera, making moving pictures in its owner's brain. The pupil of an eye is like the hole in a camera, which we make larger or smaller as we need more or less light to take a picture. The pupil grows smaller or larger

**MUSCLES OF A CAT'S EYE IN DAY TIME**

These muscles are loose. ①

These muscles are tight, (squeezing). ②

Pupil is slit-like.

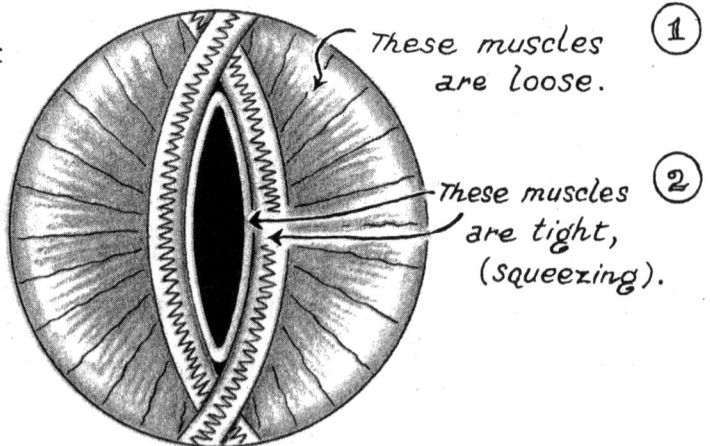

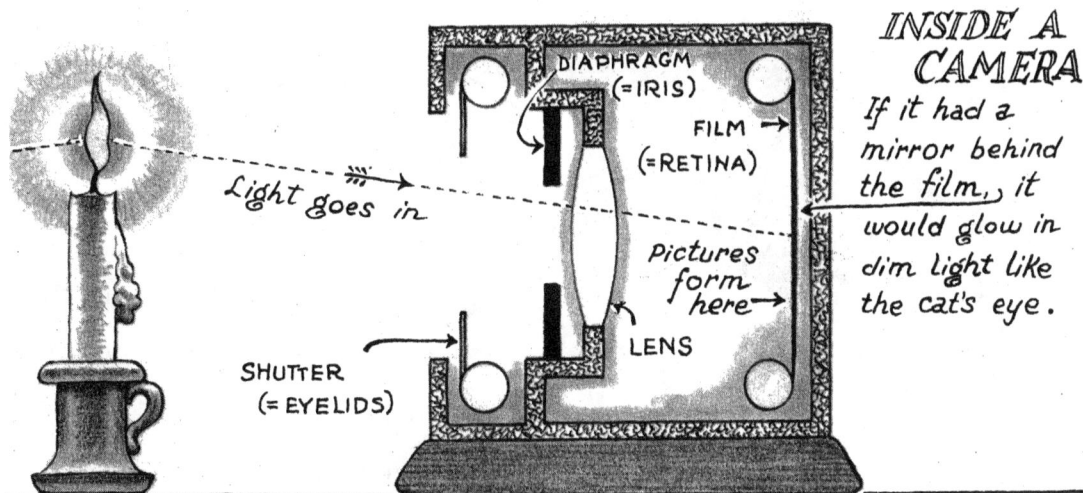

INSIDE A CAMERA
If it had a mirror behind the film, it would glow in dim light like the cat's eye.

DIAPHRAGM (=IRIS)

FILM (=RETINA)

Light goes in

Pictures form here →

SHUTTER (=EYELIDS)

LENS

as the light grows brighter or duller. A cat's eyes have especially good pupils, closing ever more narrowly after sunrise but opening almost as wide as the eyes themselves after sunset. Thus as much of the night's dim light as possible is let in upon a curved shiny surface at the back of the cat's eyes. From here it is reflected out again through the wide-open pupils, making objects a little plainer just in front of the cat.

MUSCLES OF A CAT'S EYE IN DIM LIGHT

① These muscles are growing short, (tightening).

② These muscles are loose now, (stretching).

Pupil is growing round.

WSB

"On your marks!
Get set!" etc.
for the standing
broad-jump.

So now let's imagine Tom crouching in the dark, and staring with widened pupils at a clump of grasses. He has heard a squeaking in that clump. Sometimes it shakes a little, for several mice are playing in it. Tensely watching, the cat sets his hind feet, ready to spring. When one mouse, more careless than the rest, runs out of the clump, he catapults through the air and hooks it with a lightning stroke of his curving claws.

But he doesn't always "get his" mouse. Although a cat is one of the best of all hunting animals, he isn't perfect. For he can't keep his tail from twitching when he is excited. Sometimes it rustles amongst dry leaves or grass, right while he is waiting for a mouse to show itself. Then all wise mice take warning. Yet there always seem to be enough foolish mice to furnish food for hunting animals like cats and

"He flies through the air with the greatest of ease"—

foxes, and for hunting birds like hawks and owls.

Suppose Tom has been hunting most of the night before catching his mouse. Now, successful at last, he is heading for home. He holds his head high, partly perhaps from pride, but mostly the better to carry his prize. He hurries a little but pauses often to look all about, a good habit for any animal that travels alone. He never steps into a clear open space where there is no place to hide from enemies, nor any tree to climb, without a careful look on all sides. At this hour he is especially careful, for it is almost morning when, besides himself, foxes, raccoons, skunks, porcupines, and other ani-

FOX  RAC-COON  SKUNK  WEASEL  PORCUPINE

mals likewise are going home. Things are always pleasanter if their paths don't meet. And even a grown-up tomcat should never trust that great horned owl which still is hunting.

With the first dim daylight, Tom reaches the road that leads straight to the house. But just as he stops for a scouting look, he hears an early milk truck coming ever closer. He crouches in some tall weeds as it speeds around the bend.

Then, with belly close to the ground, he scoots along the roadside. He gallops up the driveway, pushes through his own swinging door (hung in the back-porch screening), and stops on the door mat. Up goes his tail, a sure sign that now he feels both safe and tame again.

IF YOU PET AND PRAISE HIM BEFORE TOSSING HIS PRESENT OUTDOORS, HE WILL SEE THAT YOU ARE GRATEFUL BUT NOT VERY HUNGRY. SO THEN HE WILL GO OUT PURRING (A CAT'S HUMMING) AND EAT IT HIMSELF. WSB

"Oh my! What a fine cat! You deserve a good scratching be-hind the ears!"

"Mrrt? Mrrrtl?"

he calls through his mousy mouthful. It almost sounds like "Mert" and "Myrtle." But that little call is just a cat's "Come and get it!", the very same sound his mother used to make whenever she brought a mouse for him and the other kittens. Only now Tom wants to give this mouse to his human friends. Who can say just why? Maybe, because they always praise and pet him when he brings mice home, he wants them to notice that he's caught another. Or perhaps, since they give him some of their food, he thinks they might enjoy some of his.

1 box OLIVER'S CATFOOD repaid with 1 mouse

FOR THE CAT

FOR THE CAT'S HUMAN FRIENDS

But nobody is up yet. So he starts to play with the mouse, letting it go and catching it again and again. This habit of cats seems cruel to most people, for they put themselves in the mouse's place. But to be fair they should try to put themselves in the cat's place also. He realizes only one of the mouse's feelings, its wish to get away. Well, all mice always want to get away. To Tom it is no different catching this mouse the tenth time than the first, except that it is easier. He doesn't play with it to give it a bad time, but to give himself a good time, and a little practice. He is not being cruel, for he just doesn't see the mouse's side of it at all. And very soon he ends the game by having the mouse for breakfast.

SOMEWHAT LIKE THE SPORTSMAN WHO ENJOYS PLAYING A FISH,

SLOWLY BRINGING IT IN ON THE LIGHTEST POSSIBLE TACKLE. HE HAS FUN, SELDOM CONSIDERING THE FISH'S FEELINGS.

After a night of adventure, a meal of meat and fur makes
Tom very thirsty. He wants a big drink of milk as soon as
possible. He meows first at the back door, then under the

bedroom
window. He would
like to jump onto the sill,
but the screen prevents him.
So, climbing a tree, he jumps to the
porch roof, runs over the main roof, leans over the eaves, and,
looking into the bedroom, meows from there. This shows
how perfectly he understands the layout of the house from
all sides, top to bottom. It also shows that, unable to get what
he wants directly, he can think of a more roundabout way
to do it.

TOM IS ABOUT AS CLEVER AS ANY OTHER GOOD
BRIGHT CAT. IN A CAT'S BRAIN THERE IS ROOM
NOT ONLY FOR ALL ITS MANY FEELINGS, BUT
FOR MANY IDEAS, OLD AND NEW. FOR CATS
LEARN TO CHANGE SOME OF THEIR HABITS
TO SUIT NEW CONDITIONS,— AND THEY OF-
TEN PLAN NEW WAYS TO SOLVE THEIR

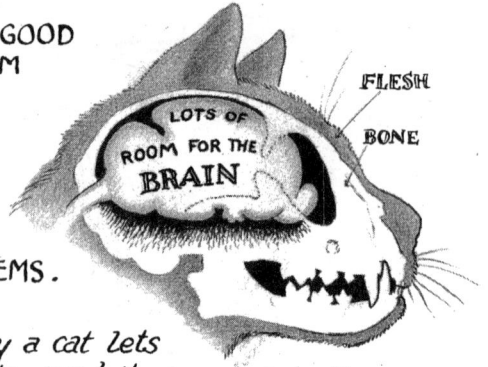

FLESH

LOTS OF
ROOM FOR THE
BRAIN

BONE

PROBLEMS.

This is right.

This is
wrong.

GIVE HIM
A REST FOR
ALL FOUR FEET.

Many a cat lets
a baby maul it, seeming to know
that it takes little human beings
longer to learn how to play than
it takes cats.

Cats have saved people's lives
by waking the family in case of fire
or leaking gas. They learn to tell
the family motor's hum from all others, and
may sit on the car's hood for warmth, or on a

horse — or even on a pig in winter. They know the telephone's ring
from the door-bell.

Quite a
radiator!

CATS SOON LEARN THAT THE SOUND
OF A KITCHEN KNIFE BEING SHARPENED,
OR A CAN BEING OPENED, MAY MEAN
A TREAT.

THEY DISCOVER
THAT THE CAT IN
THE MIRROR IS
NOT REALLY
THERE.

Feeling for
that other cat.

AFTER TOUCHING NOSES WITH A TOY DOG AND
SNIFFING IT ALL OVER, THEY ARE SATISFIED
THAT IT CANNOT BARK
OR BITE. CATS
LEARN

BOSCO

TO BE
FRIENDS WITH THE FAMILY
DOG, PET RAT, TURTLE, PAR-
ROT, AND OTHER BIRDS.

Some cats reach out, hook a fisherman's catch, haul it into the boat, and kill it for him with a quick bite. Others fish for themselves with one paw, and a few even dive overboard and swim.

OUT ONTO THE BANK WITH YOU!

Riding in on the door aided by a push against the jamb.

CATS GET DOORS TO OPEN BY RATTLING THE KNOB, HITTING A BELL OR LIFTING A KNOCKER, PULLING A ROPE, PUSHING A BUTTON, SLIDING A BOLT, OR LIFTING A LATCH. SOME ARE GOOD AT CLIMBING LADDERS, AND AT LEAST ONE FIREHOUSE CAT SLIDES DOWN THE POLE LIKE THE FIREMEN.

To get a drink, a cat may "fiddle" with a faucet till it drips. Besides catnip, many cats enjoy smelling heliotrope and violets, and are fond of perfumes such as lavender and cologne. Many like the scent of perspiration, either on their human friends or their clothing. Some adore cleaning-fluid odors.

Besides giving mouse-protection in so many of our homes, cats hold mousing jobs in granaries, on dairy, poultry, and fur farms, on ships, in stores and warehouses, post-offices, churches, and in theatres. A few have even had a part in the play!

But we have left our house-cat, TOM, yowling on the roof,—so now let's turn the page.

Look out below!

It's easy to believe that cats could talk if they cared to, that they just don't bother with words since they can get whatever they want without them. Nevertheless, what Tom's friends hear from the eaves while still only half awake, sounds very much like,

"Morrrning! Are you rrrolling out now?"

Tom has changed from a wild four-legged mousetrap to a tame living alarm clock. And there is only one way to shut

VERY LOW SUPPLY OF GOOD IDEAS

Drat it! Here I've spent 20 years trying to make a self-winding, self-springing, fur-covered combination alarm clock and mouse-trap when all I need to do is keep a CAT!

Here you are! It's time for supper!

PROFESSOR O.U. DUDDMAKER

him off. Someone will have to get up and let him in and give him his milk. Just for fun, let us say that today it's your turn to do it.

Tail stiff, Tom very happy, thinking of milk.

Tail still stiff, Tom still happy, drinking of milk.

Tail not resting on the floor

While he rubs your shanks with his face and flanks, you open a can of evaporated milk. "Pourrr more out!" he purr-meows most greedily. "More warm water!" he seems to order as you mix some with the milk. When you set it before him he laps fast and loudly, his breath sounding as though he has a touch of asthma. But this merely means he is extra thirsty. So you go to wash your face, and on returning, find Tom washing his also, using only his tongue and wrists and a little saliva.

Too tired to take in his tongue.

Kitty Say "Ah!"

PART OF A
CAT'S TONGUE
ENLARGED

A LITTLE BIT, STILL MORE
ENLARGED ~ *Each tiny
point is as hard as
fingernail or claw.*

POINTS OF A COMB

NAP OF A TOWEL

What a wonderfully useful tongue a cat has! Covered all over with little points, it serves as washcloth and towel, comb and brush. It is also fine for sponging up the last drop of milk or gravy, or for rasping the last shred of meat from bones. Like most cats, Tom is a clean and tidy creature, always washing after meals and frequently between meals. Any ruffling of his fur (as from a night's hunt in weeds and brambles) must be set to rights before he can be comfortable. This combing-washing habit even helps in the hunting itself. For his clean fur never has an odor that might warn the mice.

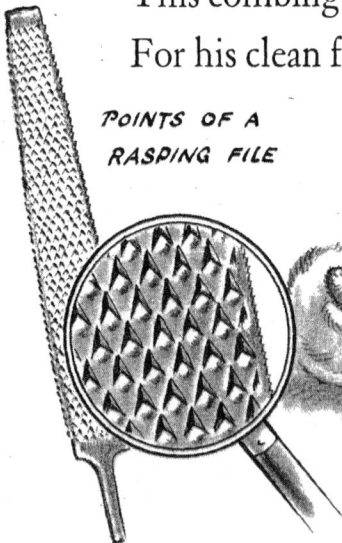

POINTS OF A
RASPING FILE

USING HIS
RASPING
TONGUE

WGB

But now the beast of prey, his washing done, is only a pleasure-loving little friend. He purrs happily in your arms, enjoying a slow ride around the kitchen, studying each thing you stop by.

He does not ask, but he *has* many questions.

The calendar picture does not mean meat to him. It is just a jumble of shapes.

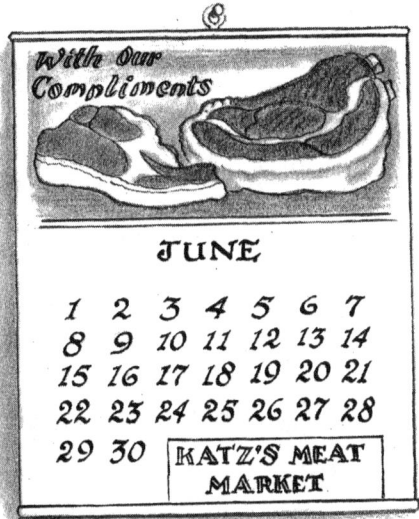

With Our Compliments

JUNE

1 2 3 4 5 6 7
8 9 10 11 12 13 14
15 16 17 18 19 20 21
22 23 24 25 26 27 28
29 30

KATZ'S MEAT MARKET

He knows how these things look. But having a cat's great curiosity, he always wonders how the things he sees may smell or feel. And though he'll never know what most of them are for, he knows exactly where each thing in the house "belongs." Just change the furniture around in the living room. He will notice it as soon as he comes in. And he must sniff each piece in turn to feel sure that everything is

OOPS! CAN THIS BE MY HOME?

*Although he has been hunting all night he still must try for that fly!*

WSB

all right, that these are indeed the same familiar objects, mys
teriously moved from their proper places. Or put his food
where he is not used to having it. He refuses at first to eat it
there. He sniffs it but goes back to the old, usual spot, meowing most unhappily. He feels that there is something wrong
about the room, for he remembers it the way it was.

At the window, still in your arms, he watches a car go by,
fascinated like all other cats by anything that moves. He may
not even notice a resting fly. But when it moves, crawling on
the windowpane, he is much excited. "Eek! Eek!" he says,
trying to make a meow small enough to fit the fly. His lips
and whiskers quiver. He actually begins to drool, jabbing
away till he has the fly between the toes of a paw. But he
doesn't like its taste or feel, and flicks it sideways out of his
mouth. He didn't want to eat it anyway, but when it moved,
being such a hunting animal, he just had to try to catch it.

Set down at last, he goes to his sleeping box. At first he doesn't lie down but sits kneading the old pillow, his mattress. There is a faraway look in his eyes. He seems to have forgotten you and everything else, remembering only a certain pleasure of his kittenhood. It began the day he was born. For he made those same kneading motions while sucking milk from his mother. Filling his little stomach and feeling her soft body under his tiny paws gave him comfort and pleasure, and then he would fall asleep. For the rest of his life he will enjoy pressing his paws against soft surfaces, especially before lying down to rest.

Presently he does just that. But it's no light cat nap Tom now needs. Having hunted so hard last night, he sleeps hard too. For he is in the tame half of his life again, safely indoors and more relaxed in sleep than any wild animal safely can be. He may even snore a little. His lips may quiver or a hind leg jerk. Perhaps he dreams by day of his doings after dark. There are no new cuts on the edges of his ears. There were no warlike caterwaulings in the night. And his paws did smell mousy when you picked him up. So we can guess that it's not a fight but a mouse-hunt he remembers in his slumber.

He may lie there most of the day, stretching his legs now and then, or standing up to arch his back, turn around, and lie on the other side. Almost always he gives a little sigh as he

drifts off to sleep again. Fully rested at last, he comes from his bed stretching and yawning. He goes and sits at the kitchen door. Some cats consider that any sensible person can see that they want to go out if they only sit and wait. But soon Tom speaks up plainly. This he was trained to do when just a kitten. Someone simply stood with a hand on the door, but never opened it until Tom meowed. Now he lets a person know what's on his mind.

He goes into the garden where the earth is soft and digs a little hole. He squats there a moment and then scrapes the earth all back again. This is another way in which cats are tidy—tidier than most animals. It is why, given a deep tray of sand or sawdust, they can be kept in city apartments so conveniently. No one has to walk the cat.

Now Tom lies in the late afternoon sun, watching the making of a flower bed. He loves the taste and smell of catnip and probably enjoys the scent of certain other plants and flowers. But he doesn't realize that the soil is being prepared to grow such things. He simply enjoys the movements of the spade and the overturning earth. When a beetle is frightened from its underground home, he leaps up and covers it with his paw, but the beetle gives off a horrid odor to protect itself. So the cat scampers onto the lawn and stops, with slowly swishing tail. He would like to play, but everyone is busy and that beetle was against it. For the moment he can't think of a thing to do with all his frisky feelings. Suddenly he jumps into the air, comes down running, and doesn't stop till he's up in the crotch of a tree. He looks all about from his high perch, then sharpens his claws on a heavy branch.

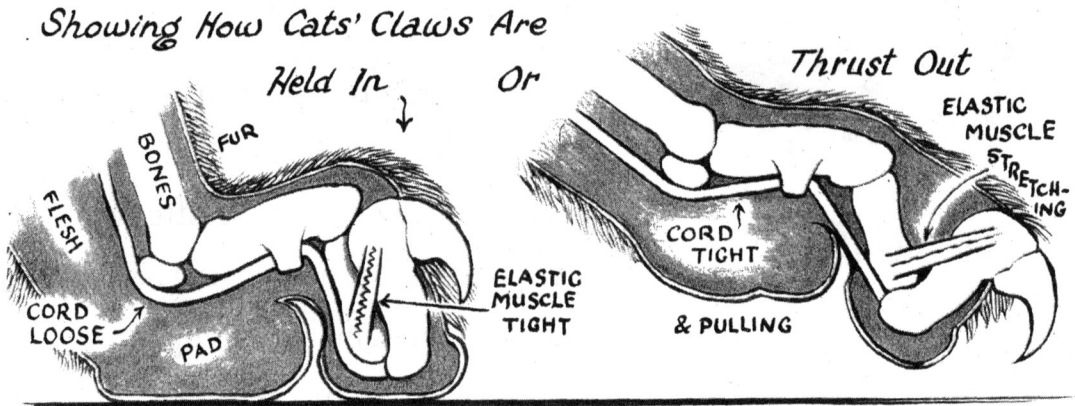

Showing How Cats' Claws Are Held In Or Thrust Out

FUR · BONES · FLESH · CORD LOOSE · PAD · ELASTIC MUSCLE TIGHT

ELASTIC MUSCLE STRETCHING · CORD TIGHT & PULLING

Maybe we should say "shortens" instead of "sharpens his claws." For a cat's claws are sharp as they grow. But they grow too long and rough if he doesn't wear them down a bit by scratching on tough surfaces. This is why everyone who keeps a cat in an apartment should give him something to use his claws on, if they don't want him frazzling the furniture or cutting a rug to ravels.

A dog doesn't need to do anything about his strong, stiff claws because they wear against the ground wherever he goes. They are his walking-cleats, his all day running-spikes. A cat walks with his claws concealed in his toes. He digs them into the ground only for short sprints. Otherwise they stay out of sight, each like a hunting knife in its sheath, to be used only when catching prey or scratching enemies. Small elastic muscles above hold the claws up in the toes; strong cords below bring them out for action.

THROWING THE TAIL

IN THE OPPOSITE DIRECTION HELPS,

ALTHOUGH
BOB-TAILED CATS
CAN

TURN
OVER
TOO.

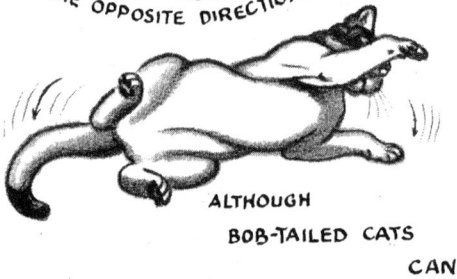

People say that a cat has nine lives, but of course that merely means that a cat often lives through troubles that, nine out of ten times, might kill other creatures. This is partly because it has two times nine claws as well as some very sharp teeth to protect itself against enemies. Also, in case of accident, a cat's muscles are tough yet so flexible that it almost bounces instead of breaking its bones in a bad fall. And even though beginning a fall back down-most, it nearly always lands on its feet. With its limber backbone as a swivel it throws its forward half around and then its hinder half, turning over in mid-air.

In coming down from any high place, a cat wants to face the ground just as it would in falling. It likes to see where it is going. But this isn't easy while backing down a tree trunk or a telephone pole. So we sometimes read of a foolish young cat being rescued by firemen from the top of a telephone pole. Afraid and unwilling to back down, it kept trying to rise above its troubles till there was no more pole to climb and it was worse off than ever.

But Tom comes carefully down the tree, head first, holding back as best he can for a few feet, then taking the rest of the trip in a leap, well away from the trunk. He stands where

A CAT DOESN'T USE ITS HINDER CLAWS AS A SQUIRREL DOES,

(AS HOOKS TO HANG BY), COMING DOWN AS SLOWLY AS IT PLEASES.

he lands, once more unable to think of anything to do, wishing perhaps for a little excitement. In the next instant he gets more than he cares for.

For suddenly a big dog dashes through a hole in the hedge and stops right in front of him, as much surprised as Tom is. The dog raises one paw, the hair on his back stands up a little, he huffs and then gives a low growl. Tom, meanwhile, his own hair very much on end, his back arched high, and his legs very straight, is trying to look bigger and taller than he really is. He spits and shows his teeth but gives no sign of wanting to go back up the tree.

*Tom is beginning to relax, though still very watchful.*

No cat need ever run if there is only one dog to worry him. One quick swipe across the nose will make the most foolhardy dog keep his distance as long as the cat stands his ground. But this is a sensible dog. So instead of jumping about and teasing Tom, he steps slowly to one side, very stiff and dignified. He goes to a rosebush, cocks up his hind leg, and then, backing slightly, gouges the ground with all four feet.

"There, I've written my name right here on this bush, and I'll come back any time I please!" he seems to say. Then he stalks out of the yard.

If You Could See the Muscles under Tom's Skin-

Muscle No. 1

This is a sheet of muscle that tightens and loosens the skin on Tom's face & neck. It covers other muscles that also change his expression.

ON THE NEXT PAGE ARE 3 (OF MANY) EXPRESSIONS MADE BY PAIRS OF MUSCLES NUMBERED HERE.

ONLY ONE OF EACH PAIR OF MUSCLES IS UNCOVERED HERE.

By now Tom looks as calm as can be. It is amazing how much he can change his expression even though his face is covered with fur. Possibly a tabby cat shows changing moods more plainly than most other kinds. For muscles moving the skin of its face, move the stripes in the fur as well. But a cat of any color shows many changing feelings with its eyes and big mobile ears. And of course its feelings show in its entire body, in the way it stands or crouches, and what it does with its tail and fur and claws.

# 1st A "SMILE"

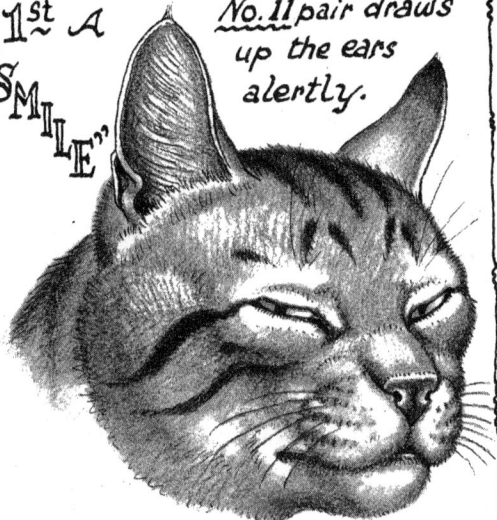

No.11 pair draws up the ears alertly.

No.1 Sheet muscle tightens at mouth corners but is loose under fur on cheeks. (STRIPES IN EASY CURVES).

No.10 pair is loose, lowering lids. ("M" STRIPES ON FOREHEAD ARE WIDE APART.)

No.3 pair tightens repeatedly, making the "smile". (Or is Tom only squinting in the bright light?)

# 2nd A SNARL ~

Nos.14 + 15 draw ears down. No.16 draws them backward.

No.12 pulls back corners of eyes.

Nos.13 + 9 draw back mouth corners, showing side teeth.

Nos.5, 6, + 7 raise whiskers and upper lip, showing fangs. No.4 spreads nostrils.

No.2 wrinkles nose.

No.1 sheet muscle tightens (STRETCHING CHEEK STRIPES.)

No.10 raises upper lids and narrows "M" stripes in an angry scowl.

# 3rd A LOOK of DOUBT

No.1 sheet is loose, (CHEEK STRIPES RELAXED), but No.8 tightens, pursing lips and bringing whiskers forward. No.16 pulls right ear back. No.11 pulls left ear up. No.10 STILL PINCHES "M" STRIPES IN A FROWN.

WSB

Tom has just begun to recross the lawn when two barn swallows, nesting nearby, take turns swooping at him like tiny fighter planes. It is a useless and dangerous thing to do, for they couldn't harm him even a little without being caught and eaten. It may make them feel a little better though, as if they were calling him bad names. He walks steadily along, pretending not to notice them. But there is more to this than the swallows seem to realize. For when Tom pays no attention, they keep diving closer. Then suddenly he turns to snatch at the nearest and it barely veers enough to escape his claws. This scares them off until another time.

There is an endless war between cats and birds. Let us think about this a little, but let us remember that cats aren't the only enemies birds have. Besides fighting among themselves, the smaller birds are preyed upon by bigger birds with beaks and claws as sharp as the teeth and claws of any cat.

Some birds eat other birds' eggs. Rats and their charming relatives, the chipmunks and squirrels, like eggs as well as people do. Having no hencoops, they help themselves from birds' nests when they can. Thus the hunting cat really does nesting birds a favor now and then, by catching a robber rat or squirrel or a chipmunk.

As for cats hunting and eating birds, don't people do that? Don't they also raise such birds as turkeys, chickens, geese, and ducks on purpose to eat? If a cat wants to eat a smaller bird, on purpose, is he so different from people who think a chicken dinner is the best of all good meals? A bird is the hardest thing to catch, so it may seem to a cat to be the finest prize. A cat, who brings home mice will bring birds also. And he cannot understand why he is praised for one and punished for the other. He will keep on trying to please his home companions for a while. Then he will stop showing them what he catches. They may think he has stopped hunting birds, but they'll never know. But any cat that can catch a bird once in a while is likely to be a very good mouser also.

Each likes to enjoy himself at a bird's expense.

Bird-lovers and cat-haters always put themselves in a bird's place. It should be just as easy to stand in Pussy's Boots, at least long enough to agree that cats can't help wanting to hunt birds as well as mice. Nature has put them together perfectly for cat-ching things. Of course, cat-lovers, in fairness to the birds, should keep fewer cats than many of them do.

Life for most of our wild birds is probably no more dangerous now than it was in olden times. For then—instead of house cats—wolves, foxes, wolverines, skunks, weasels, minks, martens, raccoons, opossums, pumas, lynxes, bobcats, and Indians all ate birds or their eggs or both. Of course, when our ancestors first came to America, many had to hunt to fill their stomachs. But today hunting is only a game with rules for playing it, rules that protect some of our wild animals. Now neither men nor pet cats really have to hunt, for both can fill up right at home.

As for filling up at home, Tom knows that it is almost supper time even before anyone looks at the clock. He needs no timepiece ticking off the hours. His clockworks are his own insides. Do his heartbeats take the place of our clock's ticking? He couldn't count them if they did. Yet between his morning milk and evening meal his heart "ticks" just about so many times. If supper is a little late he lets those in the kitchen know about it. And it isn't merely being hungry. He is hungry every afternoon, but he knows exactly when the people at his house are supposed to end his hunger.

Well, you start toward the back door. If Tom were a dog he would walk beside, behind, or in front of you. But Tom is a cat and so there is a collision, the same accident that happens time and time again. Maybe it's because cats are so used to going about alone, or maybe there is some other reason. But almost no cat understands how to walk beside a two-legged friend.

Let us say that starting off together, you swing your left foot forward, Tom trotting right beside it. When you set it down, he seems to think that it has stopped. But now he sees the right foot swinging forward, still going toward the house.

So he suddenly switches from left to right, crossing in front of you. Of course he is squarely in the way of the left foot, already moving forward again. You almost fall on your face and Tom gets a kick that turns him halfway around. Yet he doesn't hold it against you, however clumsy you may seem to him. For animals almost always know whether we have hurt them accidentally or on purpose.

Even after you are indoors, Tom gets under foot, partly to rub against your shins while waiting for his supper, partly to hurry you by clawing at your clothes, and partly because he still keeps track of just one human foot at a time. When he gets his food, he may take a piece from the dish and back away to eat it on the floor. It's hard to say why he does this. Possibly it's because, having so short a muzzle, he feels unable to keep his face clean while eating with it so close to the rest of the food. He eats more slowly, taking smaller bites, than does a dog of the same size.

cutting off a small morsel ~

Some cats are very finicky about food. Such a cat, if displeased with what is offered, may paw the floor about the dish as though covering it with earth. "This garbage should be buried!" he seems to say, and walks disgustedly away. But Tom is eager to eat almost anything we give him. Yet often, if a bit of food is dropped in front of him, he simply can't find it for a while. He bends down, moving his head anxiously all about where he saw it fall. Though his eyes are wide open, he seems to be using only his nose, and that not very ably either.

We wonder if the cheeks are so high under his eyes that he can't see something right under his nose.

H-HEE! A VERY GOOD HIDING PLACE!

CRUMB

Are his muzzle and whiskers also in the way?

He must arch his neck to see behind this point.

Then why can't he find it with his nose, which works so well at other times? We can only guess that his very eagerness confuses him.

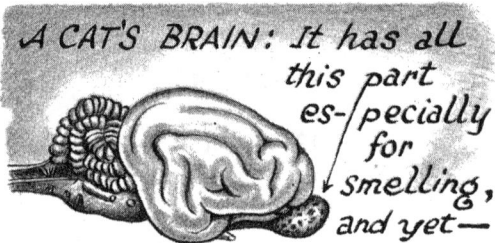

A CAT'S BRAIN: It has all this part es-/pecially for smelling, and yet—

When Tom has licked clean his dish, a big crumb still lies beside it on the floor. You point at it, but he stares at your finger. So you place the finger almost on the crumb. But when you draw the finger away he still watches it. Apparently anything that moves can take a cat's mind off anything that doesn't move. So you flick the crumb across the floor. Now he sees it and jumps after it, and supper is over, every crumb.

While his people are having their own supper, Tom goes into the living room to wash his face and wait. He has found that nobody will give him handouts from the dining table, and besides, he isn't hungry any more. All he wants now is a frolic before going out for the night. Though he is grown up now, he still likes to play, according of course to his own ideas of fun. It has to be this way since no cat can think and play like a person. Tom can't play marbles or hopscotch, for example. He can't play ping-pong, but he will bat the ball and chase it, pretending (because it moves) that it's alive and he is hunting it.

All the games a cat makes up are pretending to hunt or

fight in one way or another. In their play, kittens learn and practice these two important things that grown-up cats must know about. When Tom, as a kitten, used a wad of paper for a punch bag, or traded pokes with you through the bannisters, he was play-fighting. And now when he pounces on the moving humps made by your toes in bed, it is as though he were hunting moles in the garden.

Like a wild cat exploring a cave, a tame cat likes to creep into boxes, bureau drawers, and other small enclosures. Thus Tom enjoys, for a few moments, just sitting in a newspaper tent on the floor. But hunters and fighters spring surprises. So suddenly he smashes out of the tent, running like mad all

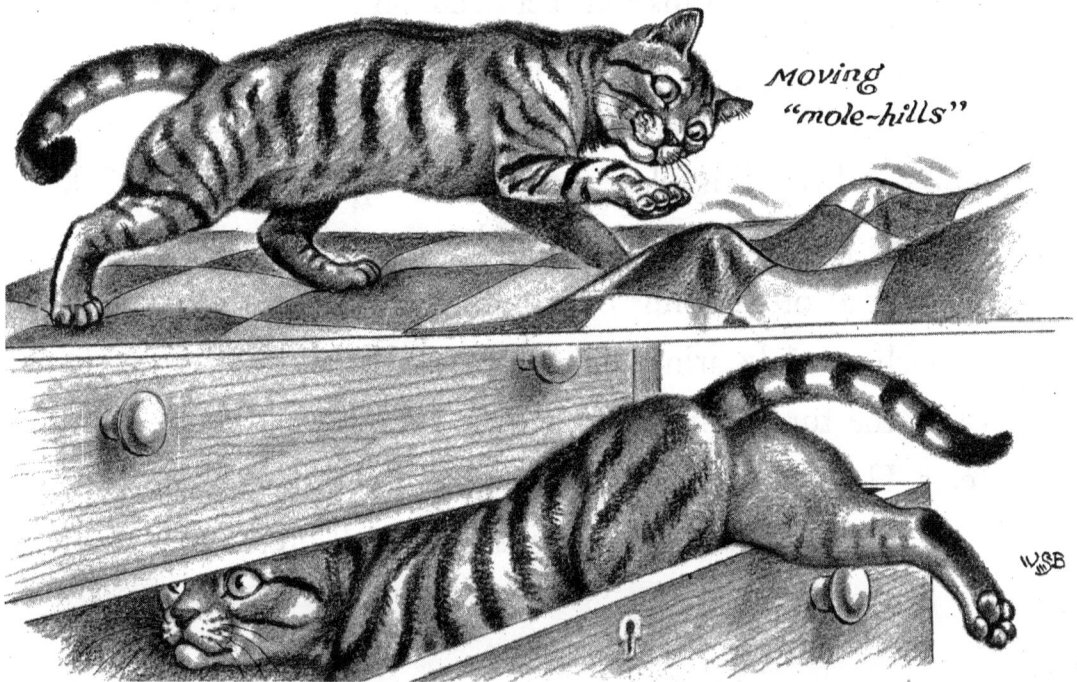

Moving "mole-hills"

THE
WAR DANCE

(legs
very
stiff)

W.S.B

over the house with you right behind him. He scatters rugs and scratches the floor trying to turn quick corners. What a surprising racket his soft feet make on the hardwood floor! Suddenly he hides, and of course you must pretend that you can't find him. He is waiting in ambush and pretty soon, as you pass his hiding place, he jumps out pretending to attack, and it's your turn to run and hide.

Instead of jumping out at him, try coming out slowly, crouching and staring like another cat fixing for a fight. Up goes the fur on his arching back and tail, and back go his ears. He dances toward you sideways. It doesn't matter that you are twenty times his size, since it's all pretending. Now

Delightful Bumps

THUMP!

HE WILL ENJOY, VERY MUCH, BEING

RAISED SLOWLY ON YOUR FEET AS YOU LIE ON THE FLOOR.

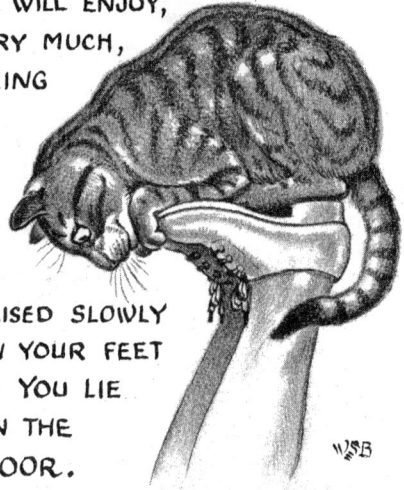

WSB

he springs and grapples with your hand and forearm. This much of you will be the other cat he has to fight. He hangs on tightly, pretending to bite and digging at your sleeve with both hind feet, as you roll him around. Like the jaws of a rival cat your fingers nip at his ears. You raise him a half inch from the floor and thump him down again and again. He likes this roughness but if he gets too excited and plays too hard, don't pull your hand away. You might get some un-intended scratches that way. Just let your hand go limp and say, "No!" a few times. The tone of your voice will tell him he is going too far and he'll relax a little. And he may give your hand a kiss, a quick lick to show that he meant no harm.

Cats are wonderful leapers. For this reason Tom loves another game you can play, a game for only grown-up cats, since it's much too rough for kittens. Bending over, put one hand under his chest and one under his belly. Lift him slightly and swing him back and forth. After four or five swings, each higher than the last, toss him clear across the living room to land on the couch. He will come back to do it again and again until you are all worn out.

To end the roughhouse, try lying on the couch, pretending to sleep. Still wanting to play, Tom will jump up beside you, rubbing his face on yours, his whiskers tickling terribly. He will walk all over you, purring. At last, believing you really want to sleep, he is likely to

lie close to your head on the pillow. He'll begin straightening out his fur and may even try to fix yours also. But if you let him keep at it, you'll have to go and wash your head yourself.

By now it's dark outside and high time Tom took up the wild half of his life again. Sometimes, as now, he doesn't wish to leave the fun and comforts of his indoor life when you want him to. So he dawdles over his "good-night" milk, making it last, licking the dish long after the milk is all gone. When you open the door, he doesn't step through it. He pretends to take great interest in the jamb. Sniff, sniff, "My, my! Is this the same old door jamb, or a new one?" Sniff, "It seems to me there's a diff—" You push him out and close the door.

# The Simplest Plan For A Cat's Outdoor Den

(You can build a fancier one
with slanting
roof etc.)

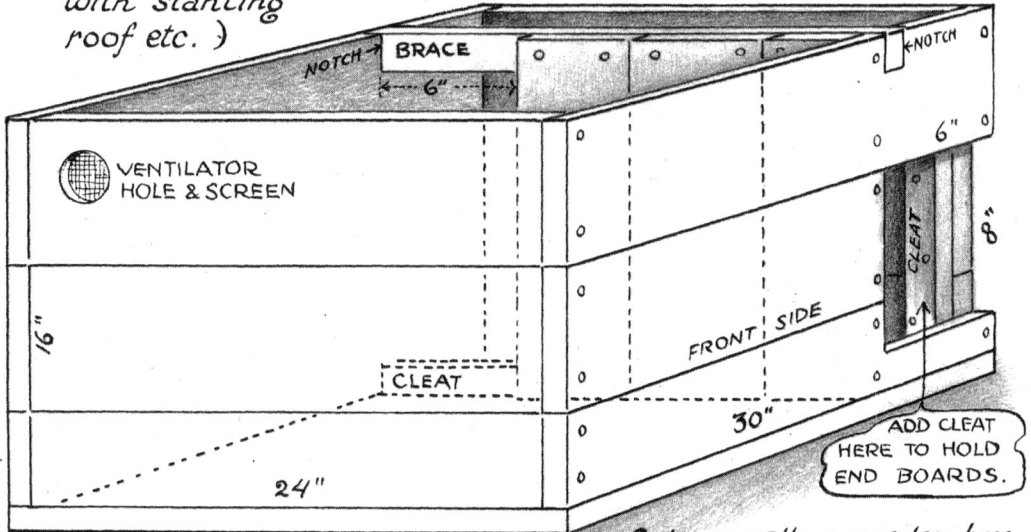

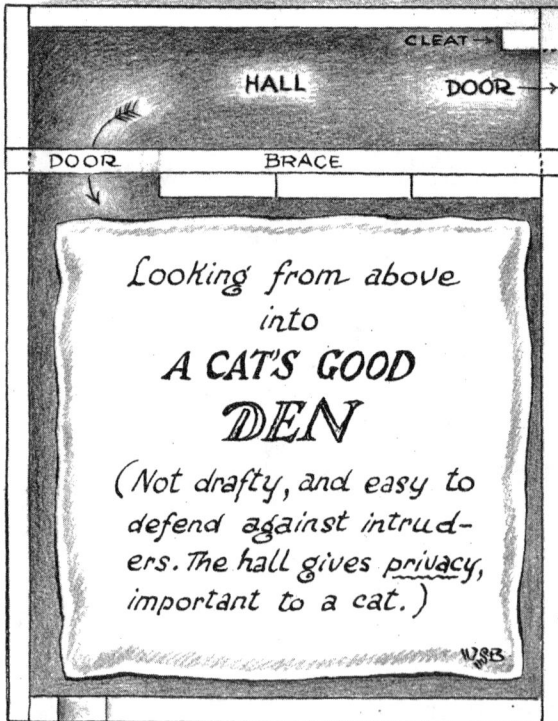

NOTCH → BRACE ← NOTCH

6"

6"

8"

VENTILATOR
HOLE & SCREEN

CLEAT

FRONT SIDE

16"

CLEAT

30"

24"

ADD CLEAT
HERE TO HOLD
END BOARDS.

CLEAT →

HALL

DOOR →

DOOR

BRACE

Looking from above
into

## A CAT'S GOOD

# DEN

(Not drafty, and easy to
defend against intrud-
ers. The hall gives privacy,
important to a cat.)

WSB

Get or make a wooden box
about 16"x 24"x 30". Notch sides
to hold a brace 6" from one
end. Set a cleat across bottom 6" from same end. Nail
boards from brace to cleat,
leaving a 6" opening between
hall & den. Nail front side to
this partition before cutting out
door with keyhole saw.

Make roof 1" wider & longer
than box, nailing boards to
cleats just short enough to fit
inside box. Cover with tin or
roofing paper bent over and
nailed on the edges with 1¼"

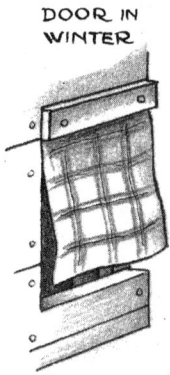

overlap to drip. Prop up on one side about 2" in warm weather. Lower at night. Line den with corrugated cardboard for insulation. Put in a pillow and an old unwashed soft shirt or skirt of the cat's best friend. Air and sun these once in a while. In case of fleas, dust with cat flea powder. Set the den in a spot sheltered from sun & wind. Hang a cloth curtain at the door in winter. A cat's castle!

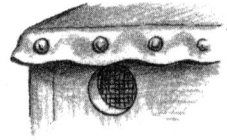

Of course any pet cat that goes out at night should have a small house of his very own, in case of bad weather. Some of the pictures here show how to make such a den. Only it's no use to make it and put him into it, for he won't consider it his own. He must be allowed to discover it. For a cat always likes to feel that he is independent, that he does what he pleases and not what someone else expects him to.

When he hears "Kitty, Kitty, Kitty!", he comes not to be obliging but because he may get something he likes. One doesn't command, one only *invites* him. He may come running, yet still turn down a kind invitation. For instance, suppose you offer him a pan of water in hot weather. Does he drink it? No. But later he is likely to be found catching drops from a bathroom faucet, drinking water he has found himself. Thus does he enjoy his independence.

**Panel 1:** THIS WASN'T HERE BEFORE! BUT IT SMELLS FRIENDLY — AND LOOKS VERY INVITING!

**Panel 2:** WHAT A FIND! I'LL MAKE THIS MY PERSONAL, PRIVATE, EXCLUSIVE PROPERTY RIGHT NOW!

One often hears it said that "Dogs love people but cats love places." This does not mean that all cats love people less than all dogs do. It means that most cats love their homes more than most dogs do. Ages ago, when all animals were wild, dogs—like wolves—used dens only for raising puppies. When the puppies were old enough, they all wandered away in a pack. But the wild cats lived in dens the year around, mostly by themselves except when they had kittens.

Today a tame dog's pack is the family with which he lives. He is happy to wander with it anywhere. The house is a tame cat's den. It is so big he "allows" his human friends to share it. But if they were moving away, he still would want to stay unless he also owned a little outside den. They would need only to take that along and he'd try to get used to the new house, because he would still have that same extra private apartment to retire to. And if ever his people had to give him

Unlike cats, most dogs must be chained to their houses.

I WANT TO GO WITH THEM! WHY DO THEY LEAVE ME CHAINED TO THIS HORRID OLD BOX?

away, having his own little den would help him get over being homesick.

Traveling in a car confuses most cats. It is natural for them to go a little way and stop to look about, go a little farther and stop again, and so on. The car does not allow them to do this. Perhaps it worries

1 in 1000, HE REALLY LIKES IT!

them to see the landscape swirling by when they themselves aren't running, but simply sitting still. It may even "make their heads swim." Some cats do get carsick.

But many a cat, especially a Tom, likes to travel on his own four feet. He likes to go off by himself on week-end trips, or on a two-week vacation or longer, now and then. He cannot tell us where he goes, but it's safe to guess that sometimes he is looking for a mate.

Now, just for instance, let us suppose our cat is not a Tom, but a Molly. Tomcats from other places come to visit her. At night we are awakened by their singing—very coloratura, though not exactly sweet to human ears. But Molly listens with a cat's ears to their serenading and she evidently likes it. Probably she also likes the awful squalls and caterwaulings

that come next, when two Toms fight to win her favor. Growling in deep shaking tones, they crouch, creeping toward each other. The closer they get, the higher their hateful voices rise. Without words they clearly curse and threaten, saying terrible things to each other. Yet some of the time they truly sound like very vulgar people quarreling.

"Run along now, you low-down rowdy," snarls one tomcat, "or you'll rue this row tomorrow!"

"You rummy old roust-about!" replies the other. "I'll run you out o' town right now!" By this time both are standing on their hind legs. Suddenly, with claws spread wide, they clinch and roll on the ground, screaming, shrieking, trying to bite each other's ears off, hooking into hide with foreclaws, kicking off wads of fur with hind claws. They break apart and begin calling names again, spitting and working up to another scrimmage. This goes on until one gives up.

The winner will be the father of Molly's kittens, though he isn't likely to know a thing about it. For tomcats are not attentive fathers. They don't care much for kittens, and after the last big midnight serenade and dueling match, each rival

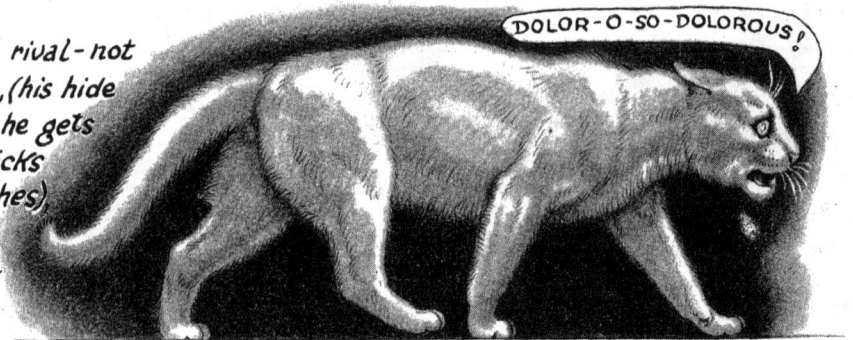

*DOLOR-O-SO-DOLOROUS!*

*Unsuccesful rival – not much cut up, (his hide is so loose he gets more pin-pricks than scratches) but feeling very sad in defeat.*

goes his separate way, back to his home wherever it may be. Unknown to any of them, the kittens will be born some nine weeks later.

*Be sure to keep clean water where Molly can get it at all times. She is drinking for a whole family now.*

*The doorway is none too wide just now.*

If Molly does not already have a little den outdoors, it would be well to make one for her special use, where the kittens can be born.

Otherwise she will hide them in a closet, or in the laundry hamper, in a carton in the garage, or in some other cozy place. She hopes to keep her kittens' whereabouts a secret. And she wants a snug little spot she can defend against all troublemakers. No weasels or other wild animals, no dogs allowed, nor any tomcats, not even the kittens' own father.

Perhaps she won't mind if we peek into her nursery just long enough to see if everything is all right, and how many kittens she has and what colors they are. But after that we must leave them alone and wait patiently till Molly brings them out herself for us to see. Their eyes won't open till they are ten days old or more, and it will be several days

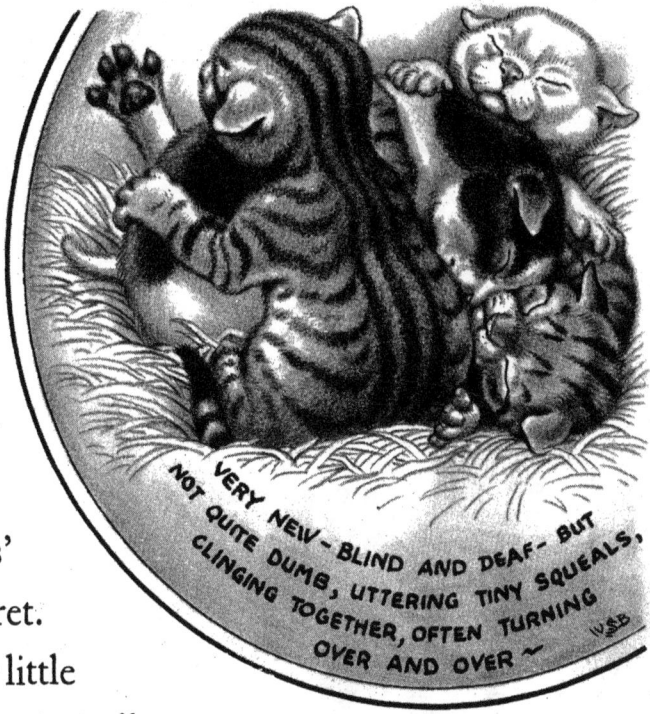

VERY NEW – BLIND AND DEAF– BUT NOT QUITE DUMB, UTTERING TINY SQUEALS, CLINGING TOGETHER, OFTEN TURNING OVER AND OVER ~

W.S.B.

A LARGE FAMILY

more before they can face full daylight.

But then a jolly show begins, for a family of kittens at play is more fun than a circus. They should be handled very little

at first, most of the fondling being left to their mother until they are weaned. By then she'll be glad to have us take them off her hands, or paws.

Here are a few rules for raising healthy, happy cats. Feed a grown-up cat two times a day. Feed weaned kittens three times a day. Feed a nursing mother cat four times a day or more. Keep a pan of clean cool water where she can help herself. Tame cats differ in their tastes but all will eat some of these things: store cat-foods, milk and cereals, meat, liver, fish, roe, cheese, buttered toast, dry bread, canned corn, string beans, tomatoes, cucumbers. The vegetables will be more attractive if covered with gravy. The boiled head of a large fish is much appreciated. Suburban and country cats can get grass when they need it for their digestion. Apartment cats can have grass grown indoors in pots or boxes.

Give kittens a chance to try lapping warm milk when they are six weeks old. Give them a little scraped meat when they are seven weeks old. Their mother should begin to wean them when they are eight weeks old. Their baby teeth come at two weeks of age, their grown-up teeth at six months. For apartment kittens, keep their food dishes fairly near the sand or sawdust tray and generally they will use it after meals. Change the sawdust every day and always keep the tray in the *same* corner. If a kitten uses any other corner, touch his nose to his mistake, saying "No! No!", and hurry him to the

A certain
troubled look —
WSB

sawdust tray. A suburban or country kitten should be put outdoors whenever he starts sniffing in corners. Or if he has already made a mistake, treat him like the bad apartment kitten and hustle him outside. Punish kittens as little as possible, don't tease them, handle them gently, and you will have fine cats.

Sick cats or kittens should be taken to the veterinary, the animal doctor. If this cannot be done, there are helpful books in public libraries that tell about the illnesses of cats, and special medicines for cats at drugstores. Generally, unless killed in an accident, a well-cared-for cat will live through all its troubles to a ripe old age of ten to fifteen years. At first, of course, all you need to worry about is the mother cat. She will take good care of the kittens.

ORPHANS
ADOPTED
HERE
M.A. CATT

WHAT KIND OF A
FAMILY IS THIS?
CAN A KITTEN
BELONG TO IT?

Most Mollies make very loving mothers. If a poor mother cat loses all her kittens, she still needs to love and care for babies of some kind. So we hear of one cat adopting some of another cat's kittens, or some puppies, or young skunks, squirrels, rabbits or rats, or even baby chickens. Sometimes several mother cats put all their babies together in one place (a combined kittens' day nursery and kindergarten) and take turns being teacher and mother to them all. A mother cat so loves her kittens that she will drive away dogs of all sizes, sometimes two at a time. Once a dog finds a wildly clawing cat riding on his rear, he goes as fast as he can long after she has jumped off and returned to her kittens.

He'll be lucky if she doesn't come forward and go for his eyes!

Long ago, when very few people could read, they really believed in witches. Sometimes they burned up some poor old woman who talked to herself from loneliness.

They also burned her cat. They thought it became a terrible

> —AND I KIN TELL YE MY SECRETS AND YE MAY ANSWER — BUT YE WILL NEVER TELL A SOUL!

SOUP

NOT WITCH'S BROTH

screaming demon after dark. (Its two-sided nature got it into trouble). Black cats were especially distrusted. They were "the color of midnight", when witches did their deeds of horror. Didn't cats suddenly "appear from nowhere?"

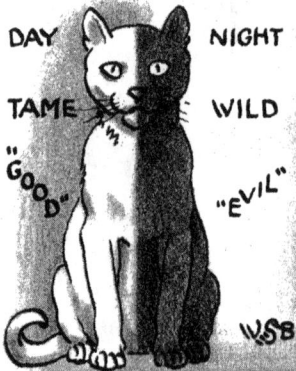

DAY    NIGHT

TAME    WILD

"GOOD"    "EVIL"

WSB

(Padded feet). Couldn't they see in the dark? Didn't they give off sparks from their fur?

> YOU MAY GET SLIGHT ELECTRIC SHOCKS FROM STROKING A CAT. TRY HOLDING HIS CHEST WITH YOUR LEFT HAND WHILE STROKING HIS BACK WITH YOUR RIGHT. THIS WORKS BEST ON COLD DAYS.

# Mixed Up With Hallowe'en & Witches.

Didn't cats have 9 lives, protected by magic? Didn't they often enter "haunted houses?" (Only people imagine spooks. So cats aren't afraid to hunt rats and mice in old, deserted houses). Unlike dogs, did not cats stare one in the eye, as though reading one's very thoughts?

And didn't evil spirits often get into even little kittens? (The poor things just had fits from improper care & feeding).

It was wrong ideas like these that mixed cats all in with toads, snakes, salamanders, owls, bats, & witches.

Now, to go on with the real nature of our cats, and their many world-wide relatives, just turn the page.→

There's not much difference between a tabby cat and a tiger. The giant cat has a longer face for the size of its body, and smaller ears for the size of its face. But truly they are very similar except in size.

If Tabbies and Tigers were of equal size, Tabbies would have: bigger eyes and ears, heavier tails, fewer but wider stripes, smaller feet, and rounder heads.

At the Zoo, we read on the tigers' cage, "Habitat: Asia." This means that their natural home is in Asia. India, a part of Asia, is famous for its tigers and they are common in the East Indies all the way to the Island of Bali. Tigers are found also in many much cooler parts of Asia's mainland. China has tigers, but the biggest cats in the world are the tigers of Siberia. They do very well in the snow and cold, far from the teeming jungles to the south.

Lions, "Habitat: Africa," roar much more than tigers do. In fact, they make more noise than any other cat, more perhaps than any other animal. They are more sociable than other cats, often hunting in family parties of six or seven. Sometimes a few cousins, aunts, and uncles bring their number up to a dozen or more. When two such parties come to drink at the same water hole, they try to out-roar each other. Many roar with their mouths close to the ground, making it tremble with their thunder. In the Zoo, one lion just roaring at the ceiling of the lion house can shake the solid floor. Roaring is not a lion's mighty meowing. A lion can meow too, but when he does, it sounds two hundred times bigger, deeper, more raw and sour than the coarsest meow of a tough old tomcat.

"Just a little get-together"—

Leopards live in the jungles of both Africa and Asia. Being smaller and lighter than lions and tigers, but even stronger for their size, they climb trees very easily. There they often sleep, and there they capture birds and monkeys for their dinner, or, watching from a branch, they spring to catch some passing creature on the ground below. A leopard makes a deep, quick, coughing sound to express itself. But usually it is rather quiet.

*Leopards are especially fond of "dog meat"*

Another kind of big spotted cat, living in both Africa and Asia, is the cheetah. It is often called a hunting-leopard because men train it to hunt for them as they might a dog. And indeed it is more like a dog than a cat in several other ways. Its whole body lacks the flowing curves of a cat's. Its claws are always out like a dog's. Unlike other cats, it does not depend on a long creep toward its prey with a last short rush or spring.

On its long slim legs it gives chase like a hound, but runs even faster than a racing greyhound, going seventy miles an hour. In a few hundred yards it can catch an antelope, a thing no dog can do, for cheetahs are probably the fastest animals that run.

ocelot

There are various other kinds of cats in the Old World which wear spots or stripes or a blend of both. In the New World, we have some also, one being the beautiful ocelot, another our biggest American cat, the jaguar. Jaguars are found all the way from Arizona to Patagonia. In Central and South America, the Latin people call them tigers. Like tigers, they generally live and hunt near rivers, and often go in swimming. Like leopards, though they are spotted cats, they have black kittens now and then. And like leopards, they hunt in trees as well as on the forest floor. So do the ocelots, which live in much the same territory as jaguars. They have better dispositions than jaguars or leopards, being easily tamed. The larger cats have round pupils in their eyes, just as we do. But ocelots, like many of the smaller cats (including house cats) have elliptical pupils, the kind that close to a slit instead of a "pin-hole" when the light is bright.

Pumas, the New World's biggest cats next to jaguars, are found from Canada to Patagonia. They live equally well in wet places or dry, on high ground or low, in hot climates or cold. There used to be pumas all over our country from the Atlantic to the Pacific Oceans. But after white men came, starting farms and towns and cities, these big cats had to give up trying to live in most of our eastern states.

A FAVORITE PASTIME OF PUMAS IS TEASING JAGUARS!

Lynxes are the cats next in size to pumas in America. There are two kinds, the northern lynxes and the bay lynxes or bobcats. Both have short tails, short bodies, long legs, and big feet. But the northern lynxes are bigger than the bay lynxes, and have longer tufts on their ears. There are lynxes and lynx-like cats in the Old World, also.

"Canada Lynx" is another name for our northern lynxes.

We may see other smaller kinds of wildcats at the Zoo, with cages marked to tell us where they come from. But where in the world did our own house cats come from? Well, the long-haired Persian cats did come from Persia. And the short-haired Siamese cats came from Siam. But what can we say of our more common tabby, black, white, gray, orange and tortoise-shell cats, and all the others that wear some mixture of these colors? Why, they came here with our ancestors from Europe. Then where did our ancestors get them?

About two thousand years ago, the people of Egypt kept a great many tawny, faintly striped, short-haired cats. To them, these cats were sacred creatures. They went into mourning when any cat died, and mummified its body. When the Romans made war on the Egyptians, some of the soldiers and sailors, liking mascots (just as they do today), carried cats home with them to Italy. Then Roman armies marched north to fight the barbarians of central Europe, or sailed to some wild islands now called the British Isles. The soldiers and the settlers who followed them took along their pet Egyptian cats.

In the savage forests all about, there lived the somewhat bigger, gray-brown, black-striped European wildcats. Naturally, every now and then, a wild European Tom would get acquainted with a tame Egyptian Molly. And some of her kittens would have strong tabby markings like their father.

As time went on, the colors of these two kinds of cats got as mixed up as the cats themselves, so that today we have a very gay variety of coats on our common house cats. Lately our long-haired Persian cats have gotten into the mixture too, so that many a common cat now has a heavier, richer coat than his Egyptian ancestors ever wore.

But all cats, from lions and tigers to Persians and tabbies, are much alike beneath their fur, except for size. We could almost claim that a Persian kitty is just a very small lion with a mane all over its body, or that a tiger is only a monster tabby cat. In any case, now that this book is done, let us hope you may enjoy more than ever the company of that tiny tiger or little lion who shares your home den with you!